Breaking the Trance of Stress

Breaking the Trance of Stress

A Guide to Balance In Your Personal & Professional Life

Copyright © 2021 by David J. Brown

All rights reserved. This book or any portion thereof
may not be reproduced or used in any manner whatsoever
without the express written permission of the publisher
except for the use of brief quotations in articles and book reviews.

Printed in the United States of America

First Printing, 2021

ISBN-13: 978-1-954968-22-6 print edition
ISBN-13: 978-1-954968-23-3 ebook edition

Waterside Productions

Waterside Productions
2055 Oxford Ave
Cardiff, CA 92007
www.waterside.com

INTRO

Ambition + balance
//
"What would it be like to lead with intention rather than tension?"

It's an old story, really. The influential executive blasts through the door of their home, kicks the cat, and screams at the kids. Pressures simmering throughout the day boil over — first at work, then at home.

Sadly, there are still objectively successful executives living this cliché. If only they could find the key to handling the pressure. The answer might just be just a few questions away...

"Do you feel like you're trying to win a war rather than make a business work?"

"Could it be that you are leaving a trail of wounded as you climb the corporate ladder?"

It's simple: you can't charge confidently forward in your professional life when you are dragging your **P.A.S.T.** with you. It's like trying to rev your boat while you're still anchored to the pier. Pain, Anger, Stress, and Tension are impairing you from a) truly enjoying the success you have already earned and b) becoming even more successful.

You're probably already noticing that this book isn't your typical corporate leader pep talk. And the reason is this: any changes you try to make in your workplace are toothless without first making changes in yourself. In the following four chapters, we'll explore each of the obstacles that are holding you back from being the centered, persuasive, dynamic leader you can most certainly be.

But first, let us revisit why you might be here. You want to be a great manager that everyone trusts and admires. You want to close more deals, faster. You want to make your company the leader in your industry. You want to make CEO.

How do you intend to realize your ambitions? There are lots of tips and schemes out there. Read the Wall Street Journal every morning. Sign up for professional development workshops. Reach inbox 0 everyday.

> **Any changes you try to make in your workplace are toothless without first making changes in yourself.**

Some of these tips are well and good, while others are quite useless.

What I'm more concerned with is you and your relationships with your coworkers. And, consequently, this means we're talking about your relationship with yourself, your past, and your P.A.S.T.

A business at the end of the day consists of humans relating to one another. Everything comes to the table: reward, rejection, dislike, frustration, humiliation, pressure. The strategies you learned as a child for dealing with these situations and emotions are likely the same strategies you employ today. This is where it gets interesting.

Rather than coach you to greater success by putting more thoughts into your head (statistics to memorize, strategies to regurgitate, etc.) we are going to try something different: to break through your trance of stress and create healthier emotional habits for yourself, and thereby better relationships with those around you.

PAIN

Chapter 1

//

Mystical, marvelous migraines

//

Pain as a roadmap to the root causes of your imbalances

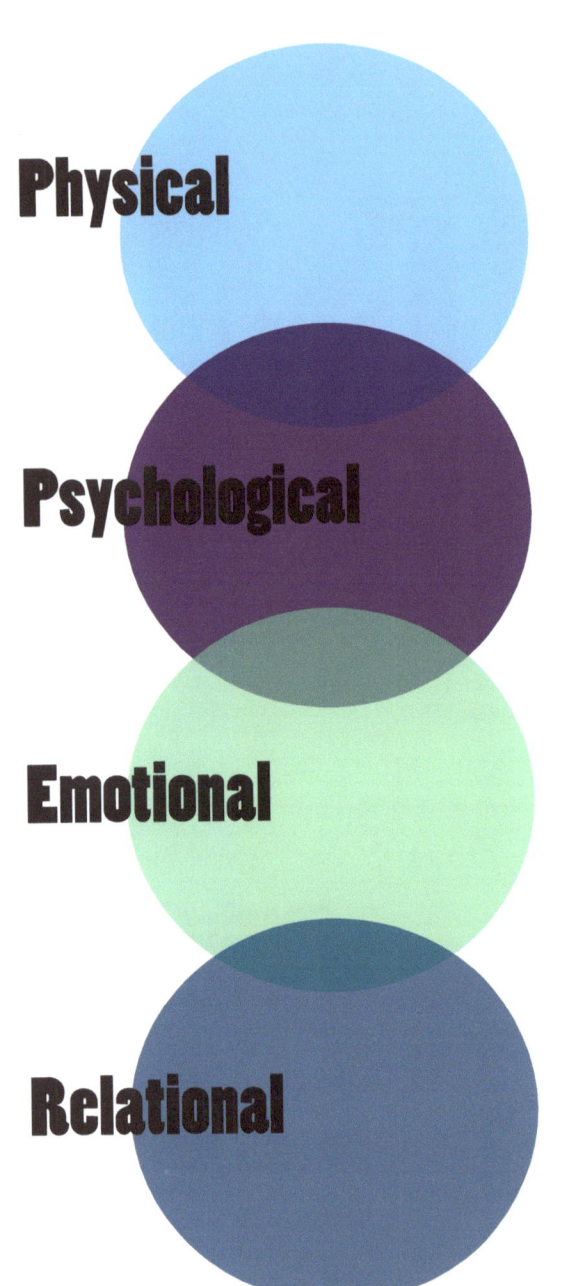

- Physical
- Psychological
- Emotional
- Relational

One of the first questions I ask when I meet a prospective client is: **"Where's your pain?"**

Quite often the response I receive is one of offended bewilderment. To the effect of: **"What do you mean!? I don't have any pain."**

But here's the thing. It's meant to be vague. The nature of the response is incredibly informative. It speaks volumes about a person's willingness to dig into the transformational work of coaching.

It asks:
- Can you acknowledge what's not working for you?
- Do you have a sense of what's holding you back?
- What are the areas of you that need to be changed or healed so you can move forward stronger, better, faster?

There are multiple forms of pain. When I ask that question, I am looking for your manifestations of pain. It could be physical, psychological, emotional, relational, or another category of pain altogether.

There's a reason why when we hear the word, our minds jump to physical pain. It's the easiest to admit to, the one our society is ready to accept. And we know that it's something we will have in common with others around us. The other types of pain? Not so much.

But what does <u>physical pain</u> have to do with coaching?

Pain is a guide to becoming your best self. It's a roadmap back to the root causes of your imbalances.

It's trying to tell you a story.

Before shifting into my profession as an executive coach, I was a practicing deep-tissue bodyworker with a focus on psychosomatic imbalances. With the right sensibilities, it's quite easy to see how a person's life experiences show up in the way they walk, gesture, and hold their body.

In the coaching context, your kind of physical pain provides a clear and honest starting point. The mind can adjust and make excuses, even lie to itself. But the body can't and doesn't lie.

What I see most often is that my clients are so focused on professional success that the connection with their body is often entirely overlooked. All the emphasis is on brain power

There is an old trope in business culture that suggests the more we sacrifice, the more dedicated we are to our work. Exhaustion is taken as a signal that we are finally doing enough. What lies at the end of the path of exhaustion? Chronic illness, physical pain, depression. Psychic suffering, too.

But having a burnt-out, rushed, uninspired workforce is the opposite of what modern business needs. Sacrificing your personal health is not actually something that's required of you.

Exhaustion won't you get you there. What will?

>> Savvy decision-making <<

>> Social grace under pressure <<

>> Creative thinking <<

>> Impressive results <<

>> Reliability <<

What you do need to achieve the above is: focus, a steady mood, and an alert mind.

These, of course, are achieved through doing what's right for your body. **Eating well. Sitting properly. Moving sufficiently. Breathing fully.**

We'll cover moving and breathing in a later chapter, but let's take a minute to examine food and posture, which are fundamentally important in either exacerbating pain or relieving it.

Eating well.

A very common type of pain I see in executives is migraines. They typically occur in those that push themselves unforgivingly and don't take breaks. As much as it seems to be an unfair, unwarranted onslaught of pain, the unfortunate truth is that in the majority of cases people "make" their migraines.

Nutrition is key, and few give it the prioritization it deserves. With many of the executives I coach, the stress and pressure of their roles overwhelm a proper eating schedule. The classic behavior is to skip breakfast and delay lunch until their blood sugar drops. Then they'll reach for the nearest thing to give them a boost of energy — usually something quick and carb-packed, like Chinese food or a donut in the break room. Beyond just the unhealthy levels of sugar and salt, the other additives and preservatives are toxic for the system.

Rather than being given water, fuel, and minerals, all the body is given is empty calories and chemicals. No wonder it reacts with violent pain.

I hate to break it to you, but all the classic "comfort foods" will cause you discomfort down the line.

The "Great Whites" — salt, sugar, flour and dairy — are all delicious in the moment, but the inflammation and allergic reactions will manifest in physical pain and lethargy. In the short term, they impair your ability to focus, due to their rush and crash nature.

Sitting (and standing) properly

A phenomenon of our digital era is "text neck." Our heads are very heavy naturally, about 10-11 pounds. When you lean forward to squint at your emails on your phone, the pull of gravity turns your head into a 40 - 60 pound weight, as reported by Surgical Technology International.

This massive weight takes your spine along for the ride. Your shoulders round and your vertebral column comes to resemble an unhealthy S shape.

Leaning forward at your computer desk to peer at tiny text also applies this ill-advised amount of weight on your head. To avoid the chronic pain these habits will cause, consider:

- Investing in a stand up desk. If you can't get access to one, find a counter that you can use. Even two half-hour periods of standing will be of benefit.

- Getting a chair that enables you to maintain a straight spine while looking at your computer.

- Hitting the "refresh" button on your posture every 5 minutes. Give your shoulders a roll backwards and glance at the ceiling. Take a breath that expands your lungs.

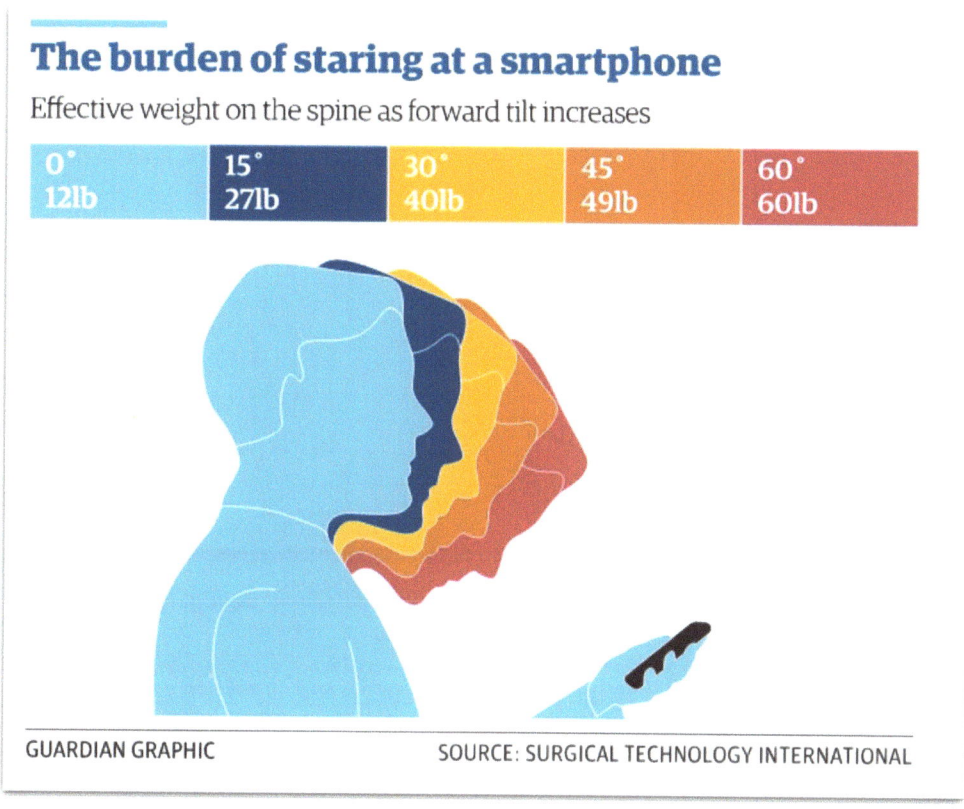

ANGER

Chapter 2

//

The past is present

//

"I don't need anger management. I need people to stop pissing me off!"

You're rarely angry for the reasons you think you are.

The following quote…

"I don't need anger management. I need people to stop pissing me off."

…is meant to be a joke. But as judged by words and outbursts, it seems like there are many executives out there who carry this statement as truth.

In the case of one of my clients, when she came into the office in a rage, the receptionist would message the members of her team to alert them of her dangerous mood. They would all prepare their defenses for a day filled with irritable retorts and personal insults. A miserable day for everyone involved. And, it goes without saying, not a particularly productive one.

When I speak about anger, this is the kind I am talking about: anger that you bring with you from somewhere else. Anger that is an attitude.

In the case of my client, she would get into fights with her husband in the morning and hold on to the irritation all day long, trying to find relief by taking it out on her employees. What we worked on was not devising management strategies to make her employees perform better, but rather unpacking the actual reasons for her irritation.

Look honestly and you'll find that <u>the real reasons</u> for frequent irritation and anger have deep roots related to your personal life (i.e. fighting with your spouse) and your unspoken emotional life (i.e. fear of failure).

To begin digging into your own expressions of and reasons for anger, take a look at your upbringing. The way your parents expressed their negative emotions and how you reacted to it will be ever-present in your adult life. The exceptions here are few.

I often think of one of my stand-out clients, Victor,* who grew up with parents that were separated, but who continued to live in the same apartment building. They wouldn't leave each other alone and had frequent, massive fights in the stairwell. When this happened, my client's reaction was to go into his room, pull a blanket over his head, and read.

In the times he chose not to retreat but to intervene, he had to get loud (meaning: angry) in order to get his parents to pause and listen to what he was saying. He had to make his body language big, eyes bulging, temples throbbing.

Learn to distinguish between the situation at hand and your reaction to it

This anger habit stayed with him. He was an intellectual powerhouse and a brilliant executive, but he would scare the daylight out of his colleagues and employees on the occasions he went into a red-faced rage. In the beginning, it was exhilarating. But as the years went on it became nothing but depressing and deeply exhausting. He wasn't being the kind of person he wanted to be.

He wasn't more effective because of his anger. He was far less effective. It sickened him, both emotionally and physically. He wanted to change.

Throughout our coaching sessions, he began to distinguish between his own personal anger and the situation at hand. Just by introducing that self-awareness, the incidences of his outbursts became less frequent and less intense.

When you get twisted... SHOUT!

Almost as damaging as angry outbursts is seething frustration. The two are one in the same, actually. Frustration is just anger without expression.

When you can't express anger, you become frustrated and anxious – mentally and emotionally blocked and physically tense. The pent-up energy builds inside, and it takes a lot of energy to hold it back. This locks up your system even further, stressing your visceral organs (guts).

So since you let out your anger (by yelling at people) or keep it inside (by judging them), you're going to have to do something else.

You're going to have to let it go. Here's how...

One of my clients, Tim*, is a very successful real estate agent. He not only negotiates big deals, he is a big deal. At 300+ pounds, with a voice to match, he's a force to be reckoned with. Good thing he's also a gentle and humorous man. Despite his size, Tim is highly energetic. He could would work himself into a lather, trying desperately to keep up with his business. When the tension got too intense, he was known to lash out at his employees and family.

This behavior caused him deep distress. He came to me with the goal of continuing to do as much business as possible without compromising his relationships. He needed to find an alternative way to vent his anger and frustration, in a way that was both safe and immediate. What I proposed was this:

When you feel the tension or emotion start to build, go out to your car. Grab a hold of the steering wheel and yell at the top of your lungs.

Scream till there's nothing left.

I sent him on his way with this new strategy, and when he returned the following week, he was laughing. "Dave, this has been the best thing! I feel so much better. I get my feelings out, but I don't have to hurt anyone. I can just let 'er rip! And then I go back inside and deal with things with a level head."

Then he paused and chuckled. "I have to admit, though, the first time I did this, I scared the hell out of the lady next to me at the stoplight. I guess I should have rolled up the window first!"

I recommend this strategy to anyone who struggles with pent-up feelings; it's a fast, powerful way to get things out of you and move on. When you keep your tension locked up inside, it just keeps circling, looking for a way out, and taking up all of your attention. I might warn you, though, when you take steps to physically release powerful emotions like frustration and anger, you might start feeling or expressing other emotions, such as sadness or hurt, which are actually fueling the anger.

Move!

Become an athlete.

Note here I didn't say, "get some exercise!" because you hear that enough.

Become an athlete of your own definition, which doesn't mean comparing yourself to Olympians. It means dedicating yourself to a kind of movement that makes you feel alive. Honing your precision and strength in these movements will animate your entire life.

Take stock of what you think you need in your life. Do you want to release pent up aggression? Join a boxing gym, or try out judo. Want more delight? Start going to Zumba classes twice a week. Need some time alone? Swim laps or go on a run every morning before work.

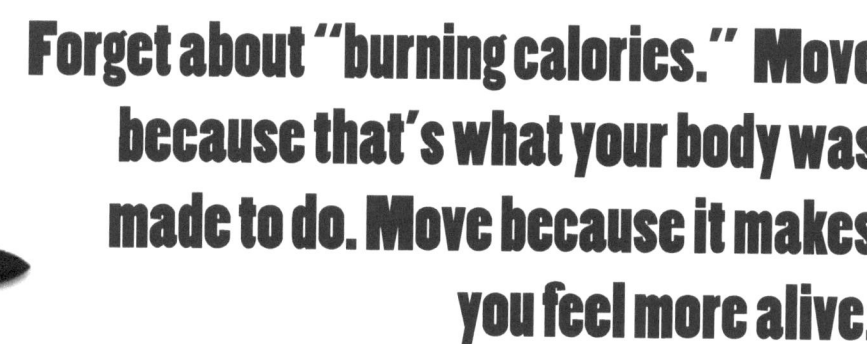

Forget about "burning calories." Move because that's what your body was made to do. Move because it makes you feel more alive.

Chapter 3

//

"I'm late, I'm late, for a very important date!"

//

Breaking the trance of stress

STRESS

In our working culture today, the word "deadline" haunts every company, threatening every employee and executive with its fear-inspiring finality. The implications are clear: if you don't finish this, you will be dead.

Even the sound of that word is enough to raise your pulse. There is already so much to do, and the fact that there are consequences for our un-done things makes everything so... what's the word...

Ahh, yes... Stressful.

When I talk with executives about managing or minimizing their stress levels, I often hear the same thing over and over again: "I need stress! It helps me perform better in less time. I won't get anything done if I'm not stressed out." The problem is, ambitious professionals often confuse good stress and bad stress.

The essential difference is this: good stress (eustress) is limited to a few hours. Bad stress (distress) never ends.

Impact of elevated stress hormones (e.g. cortisol, adrenaline)

short-term

- Enhances cognitive function
- Propels action to complete task or goal
- Generates enthusiasm about identifying and tackling obstacles

long-term

- Weakens adrenals and immune system
- Prompts fatigue, depression, and irritability
- Impairs concentration

Breaking the trance of stress

My clients think their work-related stress is making them step up to a higher level of performance while really it's tearing down their ability to perform. They enter what I like to call "the trance of stress" and live there.

Like the White Rabbit from Alice in Wonderland, many executives run around with their body language saying "I'm late! I'm late! For a very important date!"

In this trance of perpetually stressed-out lateness, they don't have time for anyone, let alone time to take care of themselves.

The trance can be hard to break; I find many of my clients are literally addicted to the chaos. Biologically, their bodies are being pumped with adrenaline, and relaxing would mean a sharp withdrawal.

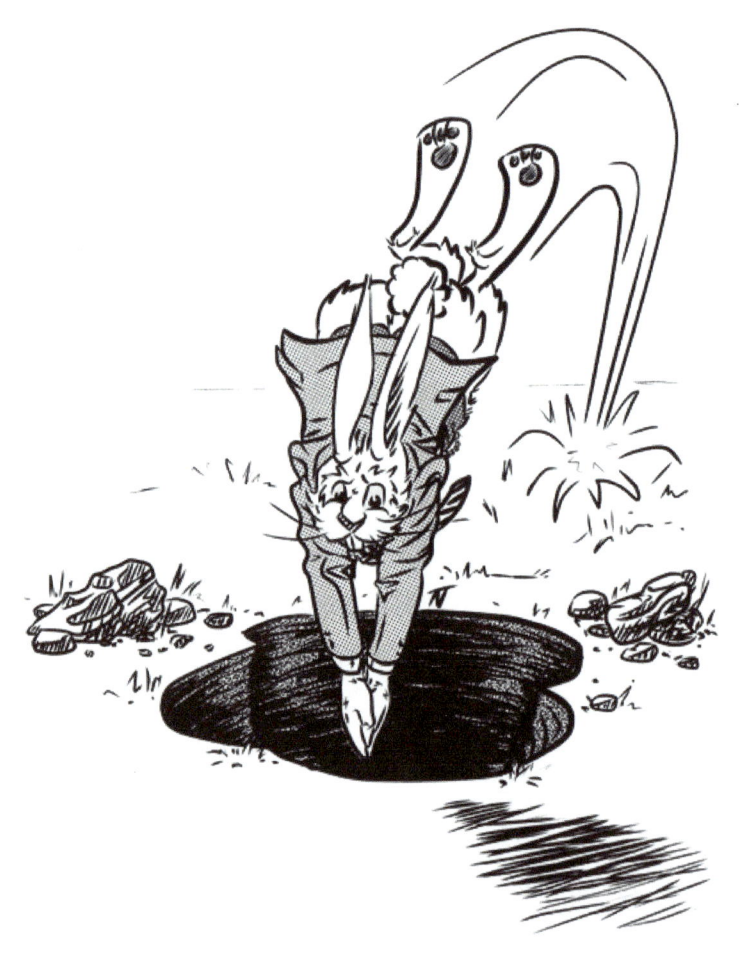

Psychologically, being stressed out all the time is a great way of avoiding critique. Rushing around signals to others (and to yourself) that you're working hard. It's a way of avoiding criticism from others, and criticism of yourself. Your body language says, "Leave me alone! Can't you see I'm trying!?"

colleagues   **employees**

family   **superiors**

Since stress is largely caused by **fear** (or as I like to say **F**alse **E**xpectations **A**ppearing **R**eal), the way to address stress is to address expectations. The expectations of you, coming from all directions.

Take stock of all the forces that are making you feel drawn and quartered like the man in the drawing. This will provide a handy roadmap for all the parties you could step up your communication with to clarify expectations and realities, thereby lessening your stress (and their stress too).

Manage up

Many of my clients have dealt with supervisors who are hyper critical, quick to yell, prone to micromanaging. And my clients have been those very supervisors. Facing a boss who is screechy and judgmental (or perhaps manipulative and condescending) is one of the scariest things to confront in one's professional life.

This is where I tell my clients that they need to "manage up." You have every right to negotiate what is expected of you and your position. It is critical to clarify this and come up with a set of goals to perform against.

Manage down

You need to trust the people you work with to their job well. To let go like this you need to establish a clear understanding of what's expected of them, both in general and with each individual project.

Rather than waiting to receive information, be a constant relay point of information. Checking in, confirming progress, and encouraging your team will work wonders in lowering your stress levels.

Manage around

A sense of camaraderie in the office is more rewarding than any corporate perk could be. To achieve this, a culture of constructive communication needs to be maintained.

Both giving and receiving feedback is crucial for creating a work atmosphere that is growth-oriented and drama-free. Set aside time for meetings with your colleagues where the agenda is to reflect on everyone's strengths, how performance could be improved, and ideas you want to take forward.

Manage home

I think one of the most important things a high-powered executive can do to create a better home life is to pay special attention to the way they walk in the door. The attitude and the subsequent interactions set the tone for the rest of the evening.

Take note of your preferences. Do you want to be left alone a little while, to transition from work to home?

Communicate your needs and desires to your family, and see what agreements can be made that satisfy everyone's needs.

Chapter 4

//

Pop goes the weasel

//

In search of a ready-for-anything posture

TENSION

"Tension is who you think you should be. Relaxation is who you are."
- Chinese proverb

In the last chapter of examining our PAST, we arrive at Tension.

Tension reminds me of coils. A threatened snake ready to spring. A towel wrung tight, ready to lash. A jack-in-the-box about to pop its weasel. The prelude to the breaking point.

Most people move through life with a degree of tension and strain, both physically and relationally. This pressure make things more difficult for our minds, bodies and emotions to function.

Tension represents resistance. Like all other things, this can be used positively or negatively. Buckminster Fuller knew that tension was necessary, he said "Tension is the great integrity." It's the force that resists gravity and holds buildings and bodies aloft. But when manifested in excessive levels in one's life, tension can look like:

- Straining to meet various expectations and avoid conflict
- Pushing to meet deadlines
- Confusion
- Anger without expression
- Perceiving constant threat

I primarily see tension in my clients as the desire or effort to control a situation. But instead of using effective communication to maneuver, their muscles are doing the unconscious work of exerting control. In reality, there is nothing about their situation that requires a physical response. This tense posture is a "flight/fight/freeze" response that makes the brain less effective in making sound, long term decisions.

I think tension is so common because it offers a sense of security. If you look like you're about to snap, people will be less likely to approach or criticize you. Tension tricks your mind into thinking you're being proactive about a situation, when really you're in a state of unhelpful reactivity.

When the tension finally breaks — in a screaming match, typically — this releases an enormous amount of adrenaline. It is easy to become addicted to this feeling of suspension combined with the cathartic "highs." Tension becomes a lifestyle. A corrosive and exhausting lifestyle.

The life-posture that will lead you to professional success and balance is the opposite of rigid. It is loose yet centered, flexible yet strong.

Think about elite athletes. They need to trust their own strength so completely that they come to competition without any tension whatsoever. Tension ruins their performance. Spectacular performance happens when an athlete (or executive, or anyone else who strives for excellence) maintains a loose and centered state and takes deliberate, purposeful action. **Preparation and practice make it look easy.**

Take a page from the athletes' book. Rather than falling back into one of your well developed automatic response programs, flight/fight/freeze, try to move yourself into the fourth quartile: FACE. Shoulders back, steady breathing, alert senses, flexible mind. The more you train to perform well in this quartile, whether it be through yoga or other mindfulness practices, the more effective you will be in a professional context.

Diagram from www.peoplefirm.com

Breathe!

The power of breathing can't be underlined enough. It is both the most basic and the most advanced tool at your disposal, and it is available to you in every single moment.

Many executives go about their lives in a constant loop of stress. A huge, high-stakes workload and multiple competing demands triggers a chemical cocktail similar to being on the open plains with a pack of lions nearby. In this environment, the body becomes tense, the breathing shallow and rapid. Deprivation of oxygen further panics the body, creating impatience. Your body and mind is spring-loaded to lash out at the threat when it finally emerges.

You need a way redirect your autonomic responses from flight or fight and back towards a relaxed state of flow. You need to be clear, creative, and flexible in order to meet all your demands effectively.

Your route to this state of flow is through your breath. First, do a quick diagnosis. Plug your ears with your pointer fingers and breath as you normally do. Consider:

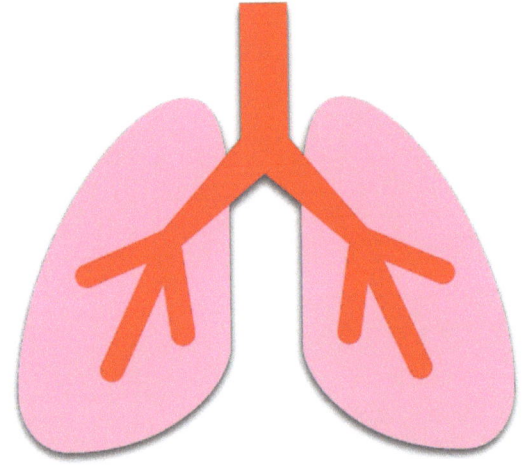

What is the speed of your breathing?

Fast and shallow, or slow and deep?

Is it rapid or labored?

Ragged on the inhale?

Do you sigh, grunt, or moan on the exhale?

What is the position of your chest? Lifted and centered above your pelvis? Sunken and heavy on your belly?

And breathe some more!

Throughout your day, especially in moments where you're feeling tense or impatient, reset your breathing with some deep, lung-expanding, audible breaths through your nose.

Bring fresh oxygen into your lungs, expanding your chest. You don't need to breathe into your belly — it can't absorb oxygen. Breathe into your lungs and feel your belly come along for the ride.

In between your large, resetting, chest-expanding breaths, you want to get into a rhythm of breathing that is full, yet easy and sustainable. Depth is important, but focus more on the length of your breath. Extend the length of each breath by a second, and make sure to breathe through your nose.

When depth meets length, then you'll be thriving. Full, deep, long breaths. As a yoga instructor once pointed out in a class, "Why do we feel so relaxed when we're near the beach? Because the waves remind us how to breathe." It's not about margaritas or palm trees, it's about restoring a proper flow of oxygen to your body.

"Why do we feel so relaxed when we're near the beach? Because the waves remind us how to breathe."

THE END...

If there is anything I want you to take from this book, it's this: suffering is optional.

We spend so much of our lives at work. While it's appropriate and expected for it to be challenging and perhaps exhausting at times, it shouldn't be an arena for suffering. It is well within your power to make your working life more enjoyable for yourself and those who work for you. The spillover is a sweeter life for your family.

Pain, Anger, Stress, and Tension are all forms of suffering, all forms of trances that you perpetuate unknowingly. You may think they are inherent to your work/body/current situation, but I challenge you to think of them as a choice. Remember that these reflexive patterns have been keeping you "safe" your whole life (at least according to your evolutionary make-up). How will it feel to let them go?

You don't need to solve everything at once. The process of shifting your patterns can take a long time. It's up to you to decide your pace of change. But it's rather easy to get started. Here's a refresher of what we covered:

In pain? Run the diagnostics for yourself — where are you feeling pain? It can show up in your body, or you could feel its pinpricks in your relationships or in your thoughts. Pay attention to where pain shows up in your life, because it's trying to tell you a story, and it will only get louder until you listen. Also: please, stop letting yourself crash. Give your body the nutrients it needs to keep you motoring through your busy life, present and balanced and able make sound decisions. And be kind to your spine — it holds you together.

Angry? Express it, by all means — without giving it to someone else. It's not theirs, after all, it's yours. Throw that hot coal at the mountain. Yell and scream, take up a sport, find the outlet that works for you, And remember, you're rarely angry for the reasons you think you are. Be aware of your patterns and dig for the real reasons of your frequent irritation.

...OF THE BEGINNING!

Stressed? Communication is the key. Get clear about what's expected of you, and communicate what you expect of others. Because the uncertainty is what creates the fear (False Expectations Appearing Real). It may be tempting to hide within a tornado of stress, but that's no way to live. Show up bravely. Communicate bravely.

Tense? The flight/fight/freeze posture of tension doesn't make you any more effective at fighting that bear, it only clouds your judgement and leaves you no option but to act impulsively. When you feel tense, reset using the ultimate tool: your breath. Bring fresh oxygen into your lungs, expanding your chest, oxygenating the blood that flows to your brain. Full, deep, long breaths are the way to unlock excellence with ease.

After you have cleared your P.A.S.T., you can show up as an effective professional — clear-headed and ready to actualize your ambitions. After all, the divide between the personal and the professional is just a smoke screen. When the haze clears, there's only one person standing there... **YOU!**

www.ingramcontent.com/pod-product-compliance
Lightning Source LLC
Chambersburg PA
CBHW040017050426
42451CB00002B/18